Coventr

FRAME *by* FRAME

The Blitz	04
Canals	12
The Way We Worked	20
The Bees	28
Rebirth and Old Treasures	36
Coventry Icons	44
Celebrations	50
Sky Blues	58
Music Scene	66
Then and Now	74

WELCOME to Frame by Frame, a journey through Coventry's recent history in pictures. In more than 150 photographs you'll see a vibrant city enjoying the good times and resiliently facing the darker moments.

The wartime bombing looms heavily in the city's history and no review of events that shaped Coventry, in spirit as well as landscape, would be complete without recognising the consequences of the Blitz.

The car and motorcycle industry has largely gone but Coventry's reputation as the birthplace of British motoring is an indelible mark in engineering history. The old cathedral was bombed but alongside it a new one was built, giving birth to a movement of international peace and friendship that lives on today; and if the city's surviving historical buildings are few in number, they are all the more cherished as sparkling treasures in their rarity.

All these topics in Coventry's "family silver" are celebrated in this publication. So, too, are the days we let our hair down with street parties to toast royal occasions, the millennium and VE Day. We look back at the marvellous May day in 1987 when the Sky Blues lifted the FA Cup against all the odds, and there are pictures of the thrills and spills and track stars that have attracted fans to speedway at Brandon Stadium for 85 years.

Although Coventry has been dubbed motor city, long before motorways came about the canals reigned supreme and survive today as a vital part of leisure and tourism. Many stars of pop have also helped put Coventry on the map and are recognised in our own chart of their successes, and we salute those Coventrians who have made us proud with their achievements in industry, politics and the arts. A snapshot, maybe, but an unmissable glimpse of Coventry's glories.

Heritage Editor: Harri Aston
Written by: Steve Chilton
Designer: Ben Renshaw

Part of the Lost Britain **Collection**
© 2013 Trinity Mirror. All Rights Reserved

Managing Director: Ken Rogers
Senior Editor: Steve Hanrahan
Senior Art Editor: Rick Cooke
Editor: Paul Dove
Senior Marketing Executive: Claire Brown
Photosales: 0845 300 3021
Images: Mirrorpix, PA Photos
Printed by: William Gibbons

▶ **The aftermath** Firemen are seen here on November 15, 1940, tackling the fire at the Queen's Hotel in Hertford Street, Coventry, before deciding to blow the building up to prevent the blaze spreading to the post office following the previous night's air raid

Terror from the sky in our darkest hour

The trauma of the Blitz that engulfed Coventry still shapes the modern city, and the tragic pictures are witness to the burden the civilian population had to endure

The air raid on Coventry on the night of November 14, 1940, was the single most concentrated attack on a British city in the Second World War.

The aim was to knock out Coventry as a centre of war production and in 11 hours of bombing the Luftwaffe dropped 500 tons of high explosive and more than 30,000 incendiaries.

Four weeks earlier, on October 14, there had been an air raid, and St Michael's Cathedral had only been saved due to the brave and dedicated work of fire-watchers situated on the roof of the building.

But such was the intensity of the bigger November raid, there was no hope of saving the cathedral from total destruction. More than 500 German bombers swarmed in on the city that was defended by just 36 anti-aircraft guns.

The city lost not only its great medieval church of St Michael's, the only English cathedral to be destroyed in the war, but its central library and market hall, dozens of city centre shops, offices and historic Palace Yard, where kings and queens had been entertained.

All over Coventry, factory targets took a pounding, while more than 43,000 houses, half the city's housing stock, were damaged or destroyed.

The official death toll was 554 but many people remained unaccounted for and the real figure is likely to have been significantly higher.

Nazi propagandists coined a new word to describe their attack on Coventry – Coventrieren, to smash the heart of a city – yet within two weeks of the raid 80 per cent of the factories which had suffered damage were back in production.

News of the destruction of the cathedral flashed around the free world and quickly became a symbol of the fight against Nazi oppression.

In all the air raids that followed, nothing matched the intensity of November 14, but the raids of April 8 and 10, 1941, came close.

During the first, Coventry & Warwickshire Hospital took a number of direct hits, leaving more than 30 patients and staff dead and the hospital in ruins.

In the April 10 raid, Coventry almost lost the smallest of its famous three spires as the church built around the medieval spire of the Greyfriars burned to the ground.

Together, the April raids killed more than 450 people, yet once again war work was quick to recover, and as the tide of war began to turn attacks on Coventry died away.

▲ *Shocking scenes Rescue workers hold sheets to hide the recovery of bodies from a bombed house near the centre of Coventry on November 15, 1940. The attack, code-named Operation Mondlicht Sonaten (Moonlight Sonata), was intended to destroy Coventry's industrial infrastructure, although it was clear that damage to the rest of the city would be considerable*

Blitz survivor Martins Bank is to the right of the image, the building survived the Blitz but was knocked down in the late 1980s to make way for Cathedral Lanes Shopping Centre

No chances One of Coventry's ARP wardens in full protective clothing on May 6, 1941

▲ **Grim search** Rescue workers search through the wreckage of the police station in St Mary's Street, Coventry, following the Luftwaffe air raid on April 8, 1941. You can still see the coats hanging on the back of the door

▲ **Ghostly figures** Shrouded in a cloak of smoke and drizzle, people take in the destruction around them following the air raid on November 14, 1940

▶ **Help at hand** Rescue workers take names and addresses of injured air raid victims

Total devastation *Jordan Well lays in ruins after the Coventry Blitz of November 14, 1940*

◀ **Public concern** *People gather around the Ministry of Information van parked outside the Coventry Hippodrome Theatre in Hales Street to hear announcements and advice sent out via a loud speaker system and a microphone on November 18, 1940*

▲ **Rush to help** Soldiers pictured on November 18, 1940, brought in to Coventry to help with the clear-up following the heavy German air raid

◀ **Mangled metal** The Midland Daily Telegraph, which became the Coventry Evening Telegraph, took a direct hit at its Hertford Street offices. This was the compositing room. The library was also destroyed in the November 1940 raid

◀ **Food delivery** People buying rationed goods from the back of a van parked in the bus station at Pool Meadow just four days after the November 1940 raid

Lost forever Aerial view showing the ruins of Coventry Cathedral just hours after it was destroyed by the German Luftwaffe

▲ **Shock** People wandered around in a daze taking in the destruction around them following the air raid of November 14, 1940

◀ **Waste land** A postman struggles with the mail on Smithford Street on December 1, 1940

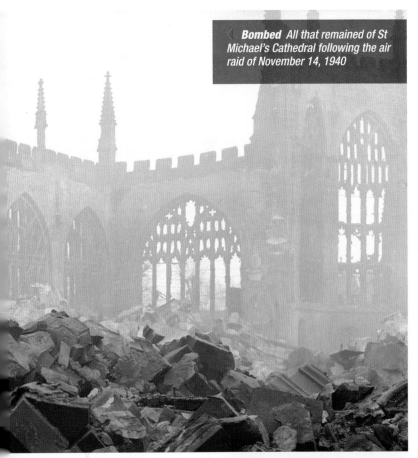

Bombed All that remained of St Michael's Cathedral following the air raid of November 14, 1940

▲ **Lives ruined** A wrecked van lies in the rubble of ruined buildings in this image, which was captured in the aftermath of the November 1940 bombings

More to come An unidentified man inspects the damage to the roof of St Michael's Cathedral following the Luftwaffe's air raid on the city on the night of October 14, 1940

Canal system that created a way of life

Canals were the arteries that fed the heart of the Industrial Revolution but which are now places of relaxation and recreation

▶ ***Bygone age*** *This image near Tusses Bridge, with Coventry Power Station in the background, in the late 1940s was captured by Robert Longden and restored by his great-grandson, Stephen Pochin*

In May 1768, curious crowds gathered in the parish of Foleshill to watch a 'porcupine', a huge roller with spikes on it, cut the first trench for the Coventry Canal.

Within 15 months, the first boats were being hauled into the new Bishop Street basin from Bedworth, loaded with coal for Coventry's growing industries.

The cargo was no coincidence. The company that built the canal had been set up by prominent Warwickshire coal owners, so impatient to tap into the city's new markets that they promptly sacked their engineer, the great James Brindley, bizarrely blaming him for delays.

Brindley's vision was to connect the fledgling canal system through a Midland's Cross, with Coventry Canal at its heart.

It was to be eight years before a connection was made with the Oxford Canal and another 12 before the full 38-mile length of the Coventry Canal was linked to the Trent & Mersey Canal at Fradley Junction.

Yet the Coventry Canal was to turn a profit for its owners almost every year up until nationalisation in 1948. In the 1820s, infantry battalions being moved to Ireland passed through on their way to Liverpool. Sixty years later Runcorn stone, for the restoration of St Michael's Church, was brought in by barge and, in 1896, Britain's car industry was founded by Daimler in a former cotton mill standing alongside the canal.

On the night of the Coventry Blitz, November 14, 1940, a vital storm water culvert was hit, draining six miles of canal and leaving the city at the mercy of the raging fires.

After the war, the canal basin was briefly considered as a possible site for Coventry's new cathedral and 10 years later Coventry Canal Society was formed to fight council plans to fill in the waterway.

The canal's gradual transformation from industrial artery to leisure asset was sealed in the late 1990s when more than 30 works of art were placed along the five-and-a-half mile stretch from Hawkesbury Junction into the city centre, the longest art trail in Britain.

▲ **Good life**
Joyce Hewson sunbathing on the prow of a narrow boat in the late 1940s and, inset, playing with her brother. The photographs were taken by Robert Longden and restored by his great-grandson, Stephen Pochin

▼ **Star attraction** Actor David Suchet popped to Braunston Marina on October 19, 2002, for the first day of the bi-annual recreation of the last working run from Braunston, known as the Jam Ole Run. Suchet is pictured with Peter Oates, left, on board 'Raymond' a 70ft wooden butty originally built at Braunston and which had just been restored

▲ **Waiting barges** Coventry Canal Basin pictured in the late 1940s

Gone fishing These young lads are having fun fishing with a net in the Coventry Canal at the Cash's Lane Bridge, Foleshill, on July 17, 1967

▲ **Frozen in time**
Braunston Marina engineer Dave Odell enjoys a barbecue on January 10, 2010, on the frozen Oxford Canal, where the ice is six inches thick. The Oxford Canal, which runs from Coventry, was built as a rival to the Coventry Canal

◀ **Times past**
A boatwoman at rudder with a decorative ropework

Frosty reception The Greyhound Inn public house at Hawkesbury Junction, Sutton Stop. The narrowboat Club Royale sits in the icy water of the canal on January 15, 1982

▶ **Lessons for life** Pupils from Southfields Junior School, Hillfields, enjoyed a term-time stay at a "camp site school" in the Warwickshire countryside in April 1995. A total of 48 of them attended a field-study course including boating on the canals, organised by the school

Twin canals The view of Hawkesbury Junction, Sutton Stop. The Coventry and Oxford canals can be seen from the 85-foot chimney of the former engine house which is now restored. Also in the photo is The Greyhound pub and the 19th century bridge, pictured on September 20, 1985

◀ **Reel living**
This man enjoys
a smoke as he
waits patiently
for a 'bite' as
he fishes in the
Coventry Canal on
July 17, 1967

Clean-up Volunteers from all walks of life took part in a clean-up operation to preserve the Coventry Canal as a navigable waterway on August 15, 1970. Armed with grappling irons, drag nets and long-handled rakes, they pulled out all kinds of household junk that present a danger to small boats using the waterway. The operation was organised by Coventry Canal Society, which appealed for volunteers to take part in a large-scale effort to clear part of the canal when it was discovered that hire boat firms were warning people to stay away from Coventry because of the danger from underwater obstacles

▲ **Sail on** The Peral Hyde canal boat in 1973 taking elderly people on a trip up the Coventry Canal at Foleshill

▼ **Popular** The bridge at Hawkesbury is jammed with crowds of visitors at the 1984 boat rally

Tourism draw Visitors attend the boat rally in Coventry in August 1987

Back to work A mopping-up crew goes to work sweeping away water from the Eastern Block of the Jaguar factory at Browns Lane following the fire that gutted the plant on February 13, 1957

When we were 'Britain's Detroit'

The motoring industry was a huge part of life in Coventry for more than a century, employing tens of thousands of people

Britain's car industry was born in a converted cotton mill close to the Coventry Canal in 1896, when a company owned by the visionary Harry Lawson began making cars under licence from Daimler of Germany.

Over the next two decades, many of Coventry's existing cycle firms piled into the trade, creating some of the great names in British motoring.

Of those, only Riley represented an old Coventry family. Hillman, Humber and Singer were all inventive outsiders, drawn into the city from elsewhere as the cycle industry, founded by Sussex farm boy James Starley in the 1860s, began to develop.

Triumph was founded by German émigré Siegfried Bettmann, Armstrong Siddeley by Manchester-born bicycle designer John Siddeley and Jaguar by Blackpool-born William Lyons.

But by the 1930s, only Vauxhall and Ford of the Big Five British car manufacturers had no stake in Coventry. The Rootes Group, which had acquired a number of the early marques, and Standard, founded by Reginald Maudslay in 1903, were both based in Coventry, while the city was home to engine-making for Austin-Morris.

By then, Triumph had become Coventry's best-known motorcycle manufacturer, alongside Rudge, another name from the early days of cycle manufacture.

Triumph was the British Army's biggest supplier of motorcycles during the First World War – car-making in the company only began in the 1920s.

Coventry, first described as Britain's Detroit by *The Times* in 1916, enjoyed another boom as its car and motorcycle companies switched back to peace-time manufacturing after the Second World War but by the mid-1960s the writing was on the wall. A series of closures, mergers and takeovers revealed how little of the industry was actually based in Coventry.

Triumph, its last major motorcycle manufacturer, moved away and famous marques disappeared as foreign competition came to dominate the motor business in Britain.

Volume car-making in Coventry ended in 2006, when Peugeot closed its UK manufacturing plant at Ryton. Only the black taxi cab, made in the city since the 1920s, remains as an iconic reminder of an industry that dictated the way Coventry was for more than a hundred years.

▲ **Happy Christmas** *The 22,000th Jaguar of 1982 coming off the production line at the Browns Lane factory on December 28, 1982*

More acclaim Workers at the Peugeot factory in Ryton celebrate on May 18, 1989, an eight-fold increase in profits and a record amount of cars produced in a year

▼ *Another success* A new Peugeot rolls off the production line at the factory at Ryton on January 12, 1988

▲ *We're the best* Production line workers at the Peugeot factory at Ryton are seen here on November 27, 1987, celebrating the Car Of The Year award for the Peugeot 406 built at the factory

▲ Royal visitors
The Prince and Princess of Wales visited Jaguar's Browns Lane factory on February 15, 1984

◄ New life
The former Canley car assembly plant is pictured in September 1981 as it became an all-important engineering centre and headquarters for Austin Morris and Rover-Triumph, as well as a parts storage area for Unipart

▲ **Jags on standby**
The E-type Jaguar car assembly line at the Browns Lane factory came to a standstill due to gas cuts on January 20, 1966

◄ **Triumphant return**
This car was made in Coventry by the Humber-Hillman Company and took Field Marshal Montgomery on his triumphant journey from El Alamein across the deserts of North Africa and on to Sicily and Italy. Here, some of the workers who helped produce the car inspect it when it returned to the works in December 1945

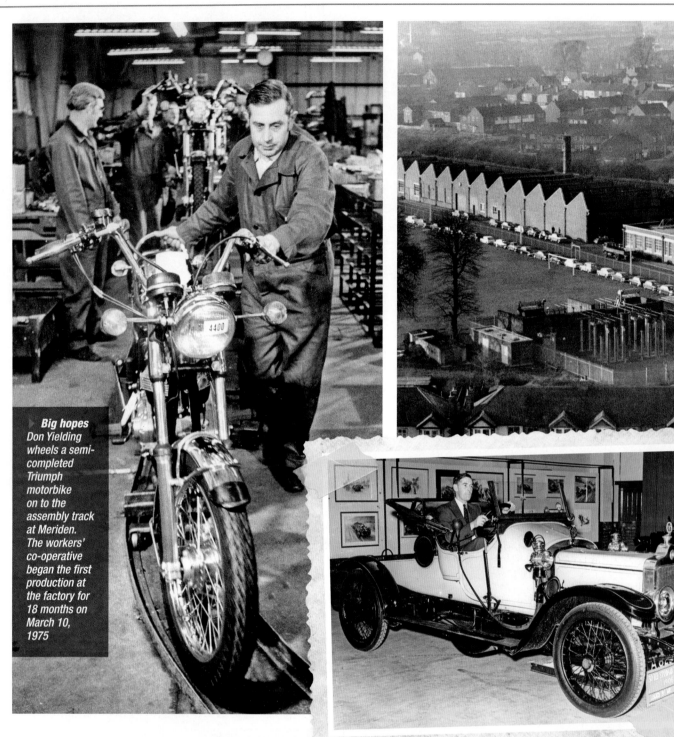

Big hopes Don Yielding wheels a semi-completed Triumph motorbike on to the assembly track at Meriden. The workers' co-operative began the first production at the factory for 18 months on March 10, 1975

New future Alick Dick, managing director of the Standard Motor Company, sits at the wheel of one of his vehicles at the Veteran Car Exhibition on July 13, 1957

Special line-up Three vintage Sunbeams line up with a 1959 model outside the Rootes factory at Ryton. The cars, left to right are: a 1912 Coupe de l'auto 3-litre; a Sunbeam Alpine, 1959; and 1926 and 1927 versions of the 3-litre twin-cam models. Pictured on October 17, 1959

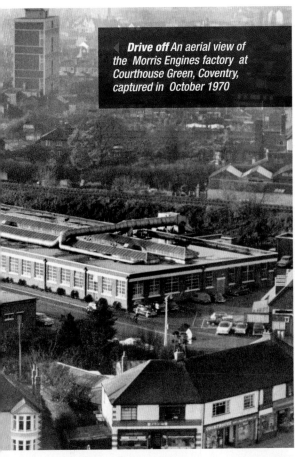

Drive off An aerial view of the Morris Engines factory at Courthouse Green, Coventry, captured in October 1970

▲ **End of the line** The last Triumph Herald, a 13/60 convertible, was driven off the assembly line to cheers from workers at Triumph Motor Company's Canley works on May 21, 1971

▼ **New models** The fruit of five years of development and planning appeared on the Massey Ferguson assembly lines in 1964 as the new model 165 tractor promised years of sustained production

Speedway thrills for city of bikers

As a major manufacturer of motorbikes when speedway took off in the 1920s, Coventry embraced the sport and became home to one of its most successful teams

Speed demons Coventry Bees against Reading on July 19, 1988

WITH Coventry's history of motorbike manufacturing it was not surprising the city regarded itself as speedway's natural home when the sport sprang up in the late 1920s.

By the end of the decade the city had two speedway stadiums, the short-lived Lythalls Lane track and the one at Brandon.

The danger and excitement of the sport attracted many young Coventry men, none more famous than Tom Farndon, dubbed "the greatest ever speedway rider". He rode on both Coventry tracks but it was while riding for the New Cross Lambs at their London track in 1935 that he crashed and died of his injuries, aged 25.

The Coventry Bees, formed in 1928, were among the sport's pioneers. The riders in yellow and black have to date chalked up five British League titles and three Elite League titles, and a cabinet of cups for other glories.

Among the other famous home-grown riders was England international Les Owen, who made 526

appearances for the Bees between 1957-73.

Although not a Coventrian, the great Nigel Boocock made his name with The Bees, arriving in 1959 and staying for 18 seasons, which included winning the British League Championship in 1968.

An England international, Boocock was the first English rider to win the prestigious FIM Internationale meeting held at Wimbledon. He was known for the blue leathers he wore and was nicknamed "Little Boy Blue".

The Bees have embraced many foreign riders down the years, too, and none better than the Great Dane, Ole Olsen.

He joined the team in 1976, going on to win two British League titles as well as the 1981 League Cup. Olsen has also won the British League Riders' Championship four times in the 1970s.

Another local man who rode for the Bees, from 1953-1966, was Jim Lightfoot. Jim, who was capped by England once and GB three times and a world finalist in 1963, still lives near Brandon in the neighbouring village of Wolston.

▲ *Speedway glory* Coventry Bees go on their second parade of honour on October 14, 1978, in a glory night at Brandon. The meeting opened with the Bees showing off their British League Championship trophy and ended with joyous Coventry being presented with the Midland Cup. The man giving the victory sign is Gary Guglielmi

Twenties hero *Coventry speedway rider Tom Farndon*

▶ **Speedway memorial** *Speedway rider Tom Farndon's grave in Coventry*

▲ **Main news** *In 1966 news of the Bees even relegated England's World Cup Win to a bottom of the page report*

◀ **Speedway superstar** *Tom Farndon in action*

▲ **Winners again**
The Bees celebrate with the British League Championship trophy on October 20, 1987

▶ **Wide bends**
Coventry Bees in action on April 2, 1989

▲ **Crowd puller**
Crowds at Brandon Stadium watch the British Finals in 1997

◀ **Modern star**
Coventry Bees' Scott Nicholls in action during a British Speedway Elite League race at the Brandon Stadium

ters' orders *Riders Joe Screen, Shawn Peter Ravn and Tommy Knudsen rev up achines at the start of the first heat on 23, 1991*

Aussie rider Rory Schlein, who was with Coventry Bees from 2005-10

▲ **Local rivals** Coventry Bees facing Wolves on May 12,1991

◀ **Speed merchant** Coventry Bees' Rory Schlein in action during a British Speedway Elite League race at Brandon Stadium

High hopes Coventry Bees line up for the new speedway season on March 19, 1977

▲ **Fall guy** A rider fell off his bike as Coventry Bees took on Reading on May 16, 1981

▼ **Lythalls Lane** The Lythalls Lane Stadium opened as a speedway track at the end 1920s, then greyhound racing took over until the 1960s when it was cleared for housing

From destruction came resurgence

The new cathedral is the city's best-known architectural masterpiece but there have been notable medieval buildings that have survived the bombs and the town planners

Rebuilding the city *General view of the city centre looking toward the towers of Coventry Cathedral, right, and Church of the Holy Trinity on May 19, 1965*

Within hours of the destruction of Coventry's medieval cathedral in 1940, it was determined that its successor would be dedicated to an international ministry of peace and reconciliation.

However, it took more than a decade for the physical shape of that replacement to become clear, with the announcement in 1951 that the architect Basil Spence had won an international design competition.

Spence's building symbolised Britain's recovery from the Second World War when it was consecrated in 1962, and more than four million people came to see it in its first year.

But wartime damage and council clearances going back to the early 1930s has left only 34 buildings dating from before 1700 in a place that had been one of England's most important medieval cities.

Most of the notable buildings on that list come from Coventry's 14th century golden age – the great parish churches of Holy Trinity and St Michael's,

the collegiate church of St John the Baptist and the city's most glittering jewel, the Guildhall of St Mary, seat of city governance for hundreds of years.

Amongst the surviving buildings, Coventry's rich monastic past is represented by fragments of Whitefriars, built for the Carmelites in the mid-14th century, the spire of the church of the Greyfriars and the Carthusian prior's residence at the Charterhouse on the London Road.

Another survivor is the city centre's oldest standing building, the chapel of the Hospital of St John, more popularly known as the Old Grammar School.

Dating back to the early 16th century are the original Bablake School and the almshouses of Ford's Hospital and Bond's Hospital, the latter much altered.

There is also stonework from 300 years earlier in the gatehouse to Cheylesmore Manor, which was built by the Earls of Chester to replace their ruined castle.

▲ *Traditional and modern* Rooftop view of Coventry city centre taken from the clock tower of the council house. In the right foreground is the roof of medieval St Mary's Hall with the tower of Coventry Cathedral behind and in the centre, the spire of Holy Trinity Church, taken on August 21, 1963

▲ **In the rafters** Men at work in November 1965, high in the roof of the Old Grammar School in Hales Street. After insulating the roof, it was given a covering of Parana Pine to improve the acoustics and reduce echoes

▼ **Gothic splendour** Interior view of The Holy Trinity Church in Broadgate, pictured in August 1983

▲ **Medieval heritage** One of Coventry's oldest buildings, the Old Grammar School in Hales Street, pictured in April 1984

Rebuilding work The large area reserved for new shops and flats, including the proposed erection of a 16-storey skyscraper block, as viewed from Corporation Street in June 1963

▶ **Cathedral for the modern age** Men at work in March 1960, attaching the keystone to complete the masonry on the 75ft-high baptistry window of the new Coventry Cathedral. The keystone is guided by foreman mason Harold Ratcliffe, watched by mason F Wilkes, left, clerk of works AW Cleugh and secretary of the Cathedral Reconstruction Committee, NT Thurston

Important groundwork Aerial view taken from the tower of Coventry Cathedral on September 28, 1955 shows in detail the progress being made with the foundations of the new cathedral

High note The Lord Mayor of Coventry, Councillor Sheridan, takes part in the first Latin Mass to be sung in Coventry's Whitefriars Monastery for 435 years in December 1983

▶ **Gateway** Exterior view of Whitefriars Gateway in February 1963. The cobbled path underneath the arch leads to Whitefriars Street

▼ **Open again** Inside Coventry's 14th century Whitefriars Monastery in 1984 after it was re-opened to the public following an extensive renovation

The way we were

The Coventry Telegraph regularly looks back with a nostalgic eye to the way we were. Our amazing archive photographs, together with images submitted from readers, tell the story of how we used to live and remind us of how the world looked. Pick up a copy of the Coventry Telegraph and look out for our regular trips down memory lane every Monday

LOVE YOUR HISTORY?
LOVE COVENTRY

Are you an expert on local history? Can you give the lowdown on things like Coventry's lost sport stadiums or the men behind the city's old car manufacturers? If you have knowledge of any specific heritage subject, please get in touch and help play an important part in Britain's biggest-ever media heritage project. With your support, we will be bringing history back to life...

E-mail the Heritage Editor:

harri.aston@trinitymirror.com

LOST
COVENTRY

Turning spotlight on our big names

Many influential and inspiring people have emerged from Coventry, from inventive engineers to political figures, writers, sporting heroes and stars of the stage

Inspirational speaker Tom Mann speaking from the plinth of Trafalgar Square monument in August 1927

Admired actor Nigel Hawthorne, centre, seen here in his unforgettable role as Sir Humphrey in Yes, Minister with co-stars Paul Eddington, left, and Derek Fowlds

In a city whose history is ripe with inventive engineers, Frank Whittle, born in Earlsdon in 1907, stands out.

His jet engine, used in post-war civil aviation, has made the world a smaller place and finds a place on many lists as one of the key inventions in human history.

Lesser known, but almost as important, is John Kemp Starley, nephew of James Starley, father of the cycle industry, who in 1885 invented the modern bicycle, a means of transport that appears to be future-proofed.

Taking the city within its modern boundaries, Coventry has produced two giants of the political world, albeit in very different spheres. Sir Henry Parkes, poor farm boy from Canley, became the Father of the Australian Federation, while Tom Mann, a miner's son born in Longford, went on to

found trade unions and operate as an international agitator, feared by governments.

Philip Larkin, regarded by many as one of the greatest English poets, was born and grew up in Coventry, while George Eliot, the Victorian novelist, was educated and found her inspiration to become a writer in the city.

In sport, Coventry can claim England test cricketer Tom Cartwright, athlete and world record holder Dave Moorcroft and a host of international rugby stars, notably Neil Back and England captain Ivor Preece.

On the stage, famous Coventrians include Ellen Terry, the greatest actress of the Victorian era, theatre luminaries Billie Whitelaw and Nigel Hawthorne and Hollywood star Clive Owen.

And then, of course, there's the world-famous Lady Godiva…

▲ **Arts and engineering**
Left, the man widely regarded as the greatest English poet of the 20th century, Phillip Larkin. Above right, Sir Frank Whittle, inventor of the jet engine, pictured in his RAF uniform during the Second World War

Stage star
Actress Billie Whitelaw, seen here posing on a bed in September 1973

◀ **Growing reputation**
Billie Whitelaw, pictured in 1965

◀ **Leading man**
British actor Clive Owen in his role as Derek Love, aka Stephen Crane, in the television drama The Chancer in January 1990

▶ *Running man* The 1978 Commonwealth Games and Coventry's David Moorcroft, number 61, wins the 1,500m final

▶ *Union man* England rugby star Neil Back, pictured in September 1999

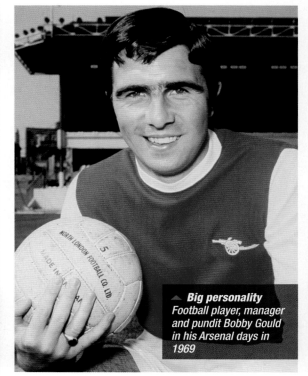

▲ *Big personality* Football player, manager and pundit Bobby Gould in his Arsenal days in 1969

▲ *Cricket hero* Warwickshire and England test cricketer Tom Cartwright pictured in 1966

◀ *Retiring star* Former Coventry and England rugby star Ivor Preece, left, retires from his job as sales director of George Wilson Industries in Foleshill Road on December 24, 1985 and, inset, during his playing days in 1946

City that knows how to throw good party

Victory day Coventry children are given Union Jack paper hats and posters to help them celebrate VE Day on May 8, 1945

IT ALL DEPENDS ON ME

AND

I DEPEND ON GOD.

KEEP LEFT

C OVENTRY defies its historical reputation when it comes to throwing a party.
Anyone being "Sent to Coventry" during royal jubilees would find a city throwing itself wholeheartedly into street celebrations and certainly wouldn't be ignored.

Ironically, the phrase probably originated during the Civil War when captured royalist soldiers were imprisoned in Coventry, a supporter of the Parliamentarians, and were ostracised by their warders.

The modern monarchy's landmark anniversaries have been the signal for huge street parties decked by red, white and blue bunting and draped in Union Jacks.

The Queen's strong links with the city – she laid the foundation stone for the 'new' Coventry Cathedral in 1956 and, as Princess Elizabeth in 1948, opened the rebuilt Broadgate – helped cement her popularity and ensured royalists stepped out in force for her Coronation and the Silver Jubilee.

Fittingly, Broadgate was to become the traditional heart of celebrations when the city let its hair down in years to come. Thousands would pack into the square for New Year's Eve to wait for the Godiva clock to strike midnight, the signal for mass singing of Auld Lang's Syne,

In 1987, the victorious Sky Blues team returned from Wembley with the FA Cup in an open-top bus.

The climax of the unforgettable journey along packed city streets was the arrival in Broadgate.

The fans took up every square inch, climbing onto the Godiva statute and finding their way onto every balcony.

Lady Godiva has played a huge part in the city's public celebrations since the first recorded Godiva Procession in 1678, and proved a town-stopper in Victorian times when more revealing costumes were worn.

For a city that suffered so much from Hitler's bombs during World War Two, perhaps unsurprisingly the biggest and most deserved party was for VE Day when the jubilant population turned out en masse in the streets amid destroyed buildings and rubble to rejoice.

▲ *Germany defeated* The huge crowd outside Holy Trinity Church in Broadgate listening to the Prime Minister's radio announcement of the official end of the European war on May 8, 1945

Street party VE Day preparations under way in Croft Road, Coventry, including bunting and Union Jack flags on May 8, 1945

◀ **Peace at last** Another shot of the huge crowd in Broadgate listening to the Prime Minister's radio announcement of the official end of the war in Europe

▲ **Flags and bunting** With the approach of victory, Coventry people were preparing for peace celebrations, and this scene in a Coventry store on April 9, 1945 depicted the rush for flags and bunting

Royal visit
The Queen and the Duke of Edinburgh visit Coventry during the Queen's Silver Jubilee celebrations. She also unveiled a plaque in Coventry Working Men's Club in Cox Street on July 27, 1977

▲ **Crowning glory** Coventry's Carnival Queen seen here with her two maids of honour on April 9, 1970

◀ **Carnival draw** Coventry Carnival procession on June 24, 1933

Taking off British Airways majorettes seen here taking part in the Coventry Silver Jubilee Carnival on June 18, 1977

▲ **Coronation special** Coventry's Coronation Carnival procession with the main tableau carrying the Carnival Queen, Joy Stoney, and her maids of honour in Warwick Road, in 1953

Float fun The Unicorn Social Club float seen here in Coventry Carnival's June 14, 1986 procession

▲ **New year joy**
A happy crowd
of young people
greet the new
tear in high-spirits
in Broadgate on
January 1, 1973

▶ **Party like it's
1999** The crowds
watch a live
band in Coventry
Precinct as part
of the millennium
celebrations on
December 31,
1999

*▲ **City history** Pru Porretta in her first outing as Lady Godiva in the Coventry Carnival of 1982*

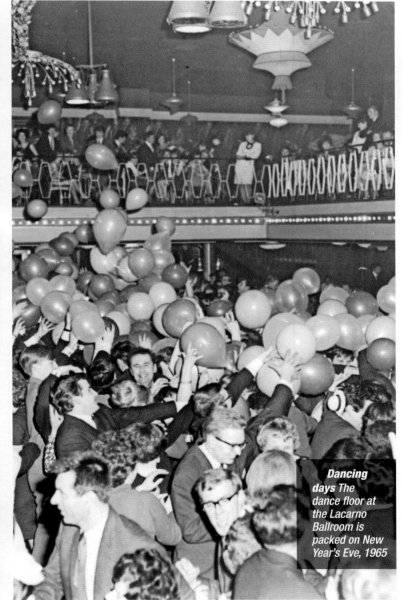

*▲ **High wire act** Frenchman Ramon Kelvink walks the tightrope between Coventry's famous spires as part of the millennium celebrations on December 31, 1999*

***Dancing days** The dance floor at the Lacarno Ballroom is packed on New Year's Eve, 1965*

▷ **Greatest of goals** Coventry City's Keith Houchen scores a spectacular goal to equalise for the Sky Blues in the 1987 FA Cup final against Spurs

Sky Blues' heritage has a silver-lining

One game dominates the story of Coventry City, that glorious Wembley win against Spurs in one of the best FA Cup finals ever

WHEN triumphant captain Brian "Killer" Kilcline lifted the FA Cup for Coventry on a blissful May day in 1987, the city rose in mass jubilation.

The honour was a long time coming: 104 years, capped by 30 minutes of nail-biting extra time at Wembley, for the club's first major honour.

But it was all the sweeter for being against glamour-side Spurs, the hot favourites.

The game was a footballing classic, rated one of the best-ever cup finals, with Tottenham taking a lead inside two minutes and looking as if they would give City a pasting.

But the Sky Blues fought back with thrilling attacking play which culminated in Keith Houchen's flying header to level at 2-2, one the great goals in Cup history.

As is often the case with football, the match was decided on a twist of fortune.

Or in this instance, a turn of Spurs' captain Gary Mabbutt's leg as the ball struck him from an intended cross six minutes into extra time.

Mabbutt had earlier tasted glory by scoring Spurs' second goal.

But this time his intervention wrong-footed his goalie and the ball looped into the net for an own goal.

A moment celebrated by the naming of a Coventry fans' website as GMK – Gary Mabbutt's knee.

The final whistle at 3-2 was the signal for scenes of celebration not seen in Coventry since the ending of the Second World War. Roads were jammed with carloads of fans blaring horns and waving flags, a city centre fountain was dyed sky blue and widespread street parties sprang up before the players had time to change.

And that just proved a warm-up for the welcome home open-top bus ride when it seemed the whole city took to the streets to greet the team and co-managers George Curtis and John Sillett.

Curtis symbolised City's rise from the old Third Division doldrums under the then innovative new manager Jimmy Hill.

Flamboyant Hill was as effective as a dashing, media-savvy manager as his bullet-headed "Iron Man" captain Curtis was as a no-frills centre-half.

When Hill arrived in 1962, he decided the white-shirted team then known as The Bantams and founded in 1883 as Singer FC would henceforth be nicknamed the Sky Blues and set about writing a fans' song, which survives to this day.

The club's other claim to football glory is having beaten current German giants Bayern Munich in a European competition back in 1970.

City ran out 2-1 winners in the second leg of the Fairs Cup game at Highfield Road; but it mattered little as they had lost 6-1 in Germany.

Sadly, the club's fortunes have not flourished since the momentous FA Cup win, and after years of hanging on in the top flight they are now in the third tier of the Football League.

Moment of destiny *Gary Mabbutt looks on in amazement at his own goal in the in 1987 FA Cup final*

The winners *Coventry City's players celebrate their 3-2 win against Tottenham Hotspur at Wembley*

▶ **Silver lining** *George Curtis, goal-scorer Dave Bennett and John Sillett with the cup*

▶ **Silky skills** *Chris Waddle is left in Greg Downs' slipstream during the FA Cup Final in 1987*

▶ **We did it** *Coventry City's triumphant players show off the FA Cup during an open-top bus trophy parade on May 17, 1987*

COVENTRY CITY F.C.
F.A. CUP WINNERS
F.A. YOUTH CUP WINNERS
TRANSPORT MUSEUM
· COVENTRY ·
1987   1987

▲ Here we go
Cyrille Regis, centre, celebrates scoring in the 3-0 win against Bolton in the FA Cup third round on January 10, 1987

◀ Marching to Wembley
Sky Blues fans hold up their Union Jack flag with 'Coventry' written on it during the Sky Blues' 1-0 win against Stoke City in the FA Cup fifth round clash on February 21, 1987

▲ **Meet the new boss** Noel Cantwell is introduced by Jimmy Hill as Coventry's new manager on October 15, 1967

▶ **Five-star show** Coventry City fans enjoy watching their team beat Crewe 5-1 in a Division Three match at Highfield Road on September 17, 1963

▲ **Local derby** *Roger Van Gool, Coventry's Belgian striker, is tightly marked by Gary Pendrey during league match against West Brom on March 8, 1980*

▶ **Club stalwart** *George Curtis raises his hands in elation as Coventry City beat Wolves 3-1 at Highfiield Road on April 29, 1967*

◀ **Man of the Day** *Jimmy Hill at Highfield Road following the announcement of his appointment as chairman of Coventry City on May 12,1980*

▶ **Big atmosphere** *Music fans watching The Specials at The Butts stadium on June 22, 1981*

The soundtrack to life in Coventry

The city has played a massively influential role on the sound of the British charts, from 2 Tone to Pete Waterman's bubble-gum pop

THE old Locarno, aka 'The Rockhouse,' has a claim to be the UK's Motor City Hit Factory. A live version of Chuck Berry's My-ding-a-ling recorded at a student concert there gave the American his biggest selling – and many say his worst – record, making number one in 1972.

The dance hall, now Coventry Library, was also the training ground for a fledgling DJ called Pete Waterman.

Coventry's godfather of pop is today credited with 22 number ones and worldwide sales of 500 million discs.

He was "the ears" of the all conquering Stock-Aitken-Waterman partnership that launched artists like Kylie Minogue, Jason Donovan and Rick Astley.

Before he shot to fame, it was The Specials who were synonymous with the name of Coventry, largely through their haunting number one single Ghost Town in 1981.

The band's success was built on a raucous blend of punk and ska, launched under their own 2 Tone label, reflecting their multi-cultural ethos.

The city's other major 2 Tone act, Selecter, fronted by rude girl Pauline Black, also scored many chart hits, notably the 1979 classic On My Radio.

The start of the 1980s was also a golden time for Coventry singer/actress Hazel O'Connor with hit singles including Eighth Day (1980, number five) and Will You (number eight, 1981) after her breakthrough starring in the film Breaking Glass.

Today, the city's most successful band is undoubtedly Indie rockers The Enemy, who exploded on the scene in 2007 with a number one album, We'll Live And Die In These Towns.

The trio are a major draw at gigs and festivals in the UK and have made three best-selling UK albums.

Other successful chart acts from Coventry include King (Love and Pride, number two in 1984), Lieutenant Pigeon (number one in 1972 with Mouldy Old Dough) and Don Fardon (Indian Reservation, a top 10 hit in the USA in 1968 and in the UK in 1970).

And let's not forget a couple of Coventry-born crooners who led the way: Frank Ifield, whose hits included a number one in 1962 with I Remember You and Vince Hill, who took Edelweiss to number two in 1967.

▲ *Chip off the old block* The Specials outside a chip shop in Bishop Street, Coventry, in 1980

▼ **On stage** Pauline Black from The Selecter in concert at the Tic Toc club in Coventry on July 6, 1991

Fun time Charlie Anderson, guitarist with The Selecter, joined children on a 2 Tone float during Coventry Carnival on June 14, 1980

▲ **Influential producer** Singer Rick Astley with record producers Mike Stock, Matt Aitken and Coventry's Pete Waterman, right, pictured in December 1987

▼ **Stage star** Singer Vince Hill, who was performing in Tonight's The Night at the Talk Of The Town theatre, is seen talking to his wife on the phone back stage during a break in rehearsals on September 23, 1971. She was expecting their first child within the next few days

▲ **Local heroes return** The Specials in Coventry on November 29, 1979 to play before more than 2,000 fans. The fans packed Tiffany's in the Precinct for the group's final concert of a 48-venue tour of Britain

▲ *Stage presence*
Hazel O'Connor performs on stage at the outdoor concert in aid of racial harmony at The Butts stadium in Coventry on June 22, 1981

▶ *Charity gig*
Terry Hall and The Colourfield performed on stage at Lanchester Polytechnic in the 'Cov Aid' event to help feed starving children in Africa. It was the hometown debut for the Colourfield on October 21, 1985

▲ **Back home** *2 Tone stars were reunited in March 1991 in an effort to save the hard-up Tic Toc club. Ex-Specials members Lynval Golding and Jerry Dammers took to the stage in a sell-out benefit evening to raise cash for the Hillfields venue. The pair, along with former Selector member Noel Davies, joined Ska group The Cosmos for the gig. Back row, from left, are Jerry Dammers, Roddy Radiation, Lynval Golding. Front row, 2 Tone record producer Roger Lomas with ex-Selecter members Noel Davies and Charlie Bainbridge*

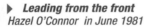

▶ **Leading from the front**
Hazel O'Connor in June 1981

◀ **Musical heritage** *Hazel O'Connor and Lieutenant Pigeon frontman Rob Woodward receiving their plaques for Coventry's Wall of Fame from Pete Clemens, left, on December 5, 2011*

THIS WAY TO
George
Best
Rogue
MEN'S HIGH FASHIONS
CHILDREN'S FASHIONS
GENT'S HAIR STYLISTS
(NO APPOINTMENT NEEDED).

Best man *Don Fardon, right, seen here with George Best, left, was the frontman for The Sorrows in the 1960s and enjoyed solo success in the 1970s*

▲ **Metal stars** *Members of Napalm Death, the thrash band whose frontman was Lee Dorrian, right, from Wood End, pictured in 1989*

◀ *Chart* **success** *King, from left Tony Hall, Jim Lantsbery, Paul King and Mick Roberts. Pictured March 24, 1985*

◀ **Current crop** Coventry band The Enemy. From left, Liam Watt, Tom Clarke and Andy Hopkins

▲ **Chart topper** Singer Frank Ifield seen here posing for the Reveille newspaper for a fashion feature in 1962. Ifield achieved considerable success in the first half of 1960s, reaching the number one spot in the UK singles chart four times between 1962 and 1963

◀ **Indie star** Singer Tracy Cattell, of Coventry group The Primitives, with youngsters at the opening of a wildlife exhibition at the Herbert Art Gallery on August 25, 1989

Incredible difference The Coventry City players warm up at the impressive Ricoh Arena while, inset, memories begin to fade of the Foleshill gasworks and abandoned land that used to occupy the same area just a few years earlier

A city transformed by force of progress

Coventry has undergone massive changes in the past 70 years and not all of it due to the terrible damage inflicted during the Blitz. Massive building projects have revolutionised our city

FEW city centres can have had so many dramatic changes to their landscape as Coventry.

Hitler's bombs were responsible for destroying many of the centre's medieval buildings during the war but the local authority's development of major thoroughfares like Trinity Street and Corporation Street in the late 1930s had also taken a toll.

And the city continues to change. In the past decade, the much-loved Coventry Theatre was demolished to make way for Millennium Place and an expanded Coventry Transport Museum.

The city's heart, Broadgate, once a traditional meeting point and a hub for taxis and buses, was controversially pedestrianised in 2012.

The square had undergone many transformations since its opening by Princess Elizabeth in 1948 and opinion is divided on the latest facelift.

Few would argue that the old Foleshill gasworks should have been kept.

The once-derelict site is now dominated by the Ricoh Arena, home of the Sky Blues and thriving as a rock concert venue.

The present owners of the football club say they intend leaving the stadium so a question mark hangs over its future use.

The city's Pool Meadow bus station takes its name from what it once was – a meadow with a pool which fed into the River Sherbourne. The site in the early years of the 20th century was used for fairs but has since had at least three bus stations on it, the latest version opening in 1994.

Nearby is the Old Fire Station, built in 1902, and a working unit until the mid-1970, now converted for use as a bar and restaurant.

The 1950s trend-setting shopping precinct designed by Donald Gibson remains the largest post-war redevelopment.

It, too, has evolved with buildings added or taken away. The consensus now is that it's time has gone and there are plans afoot to redesign the whole of the south side.

Outside the city centre, the changes are most evident in the sites where huge factories once stood.

The Standard Triumph car works at Canley is now a shopping and business park, known unaffectionately as 'malfunction junction' because of the confusing traffic arrangements.

The Peugeot plant at Ryton is flattened and will be a warehouse and distribution centre; its engine plant in Stoke, Coventry is a new housing estate.

The same fate befell what was the home of the British-made tractor, Massey Ferguson. Its Banner Lane plant has given way to modern housing.

Contemporary image West Orchards and Smithford Way in the modern era

◀ As it is Corporation Street in the modern age

▲ Giant development A modern view of Corporation Street with the Old Grammar School on the right

◀ Rooftop view This unusual view of Corporation Street was taken on May 1, 1963 as workmen repaired the roof of the city's most ancient building, the Old Grammar School in Hales Street, which dates back to 1153

▲ **Armistice Day**
Inspector Langford and PC 150 Smith are standing in the road to halt the traffic while the two minutes' silence takes place in Broadgate, November 11, 1929

Eyesore *Prefab shops occupy one side of Broadgate in Coventry city centre. They were erected in 1947 as temporary shops but, as seen in December 1971, they remained in place for many years*

▲ *Mini record* Hundreds of honking, hooting Minis delighted crowds by turning the centre of Coventry into a traffic warden's nightmare. Around 1,400 vehicles from across the country took part in what was thought to be the world's largest Mini traffic jam in July 1985

▼ *Great leap forward* Open space and large shops, the modern take on Broadgate

▲ **There she goes** Images of the Massey Ferguson tower in Tile Hill, Banner Lane, as it is demolished in a controlled explosion on July 8, 2012

▶ **Industrial heart** An aerial view of the Massey Ferguson factory and assembly lines at Banner Lane on July 15, 1997

◀ **Last tractor** Inset, workers at Massey Ferguson celebrate the 517,651st and last TE 20 tractor to roll off the assembly line at Banner Lane in June 1956

▼ **Towering ambition** The Massey Ferguson tower block and factory gates in Banner Lane on January 12, 1981

Modern look Banner Lane as it is today, with a new housing estate developed on it

Changing face Henry Davidson's Banner Court development in Banner Lane